This book belongs to :

Alphabet
TRACE THE LETTERS

A - Z

ankylosaurs

ankylosaurs

a a a a a a a

A A A A A A A

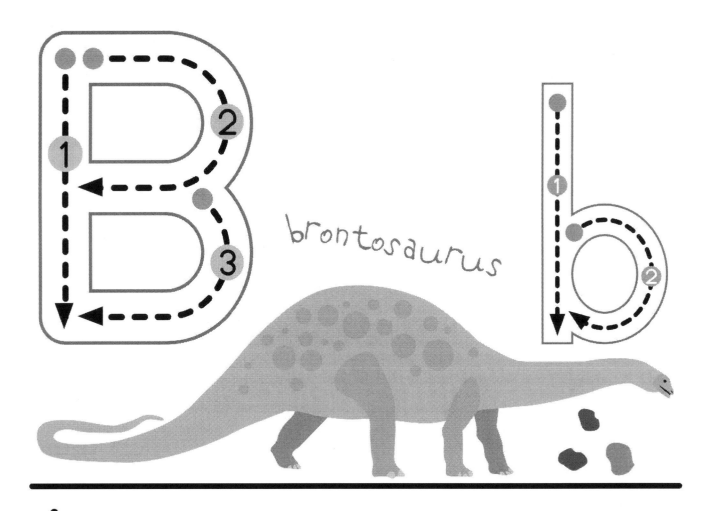

brontosaurus

brontosaurus

b b b b b b b

B B B B B B

caudipteryx

caudipteryx

c c c c c c c

C C C C C C

dimetrodon

dimetrodon

d d d d d d d

D D D D D D

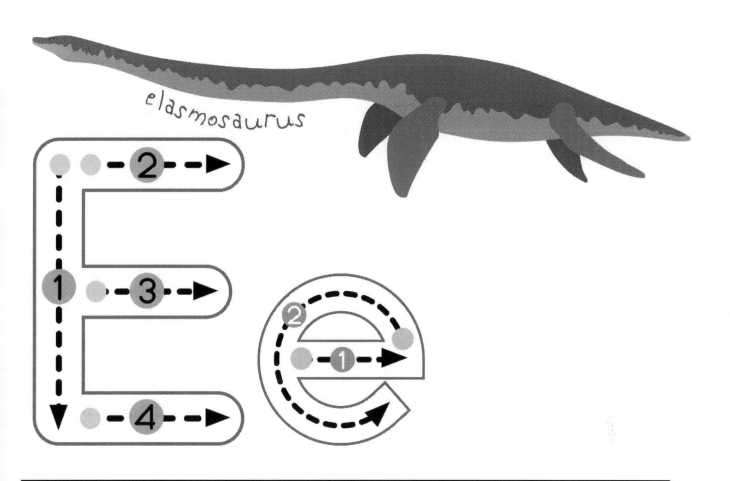

elasmosaurus

elasmosaurus

e e e e e e e

E E E E E E

fukuisaurus

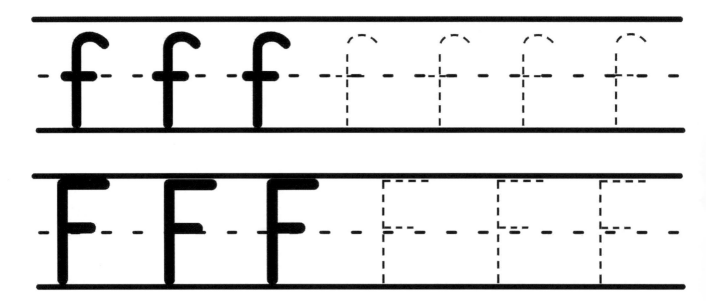

gorgosaurus

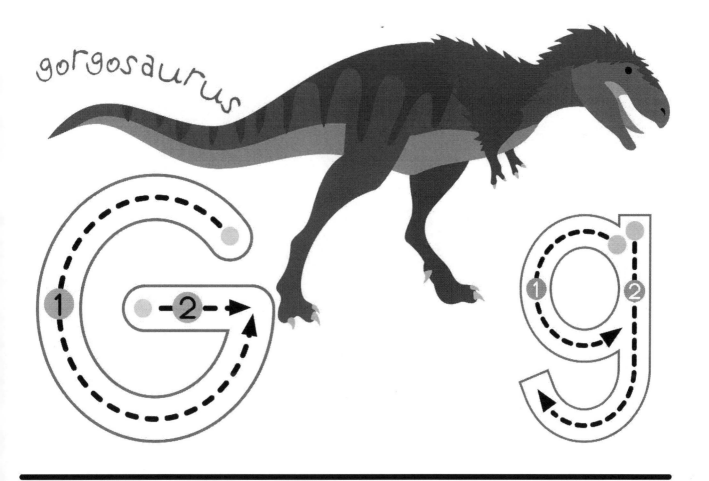

gorgosaurus

g g g g g g g

G G G G G G G

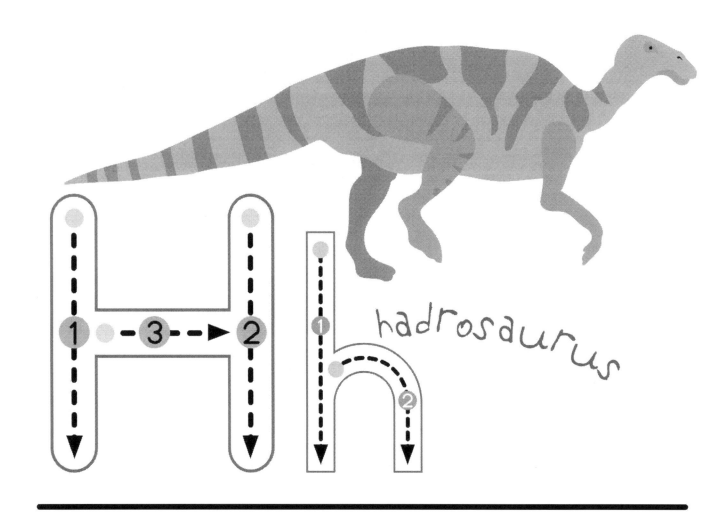

hadrosaurus

hadrosaurus

h h h h h h h

H H H H H H H

iguanodon

iguanodon

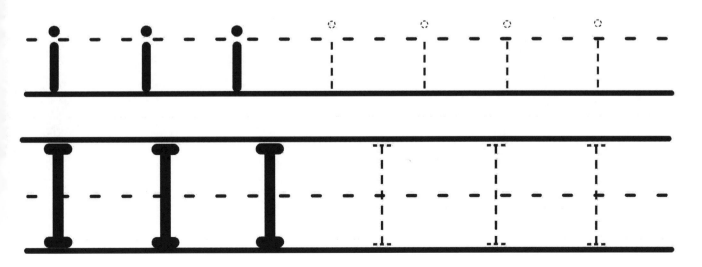

jobaria

jobaria

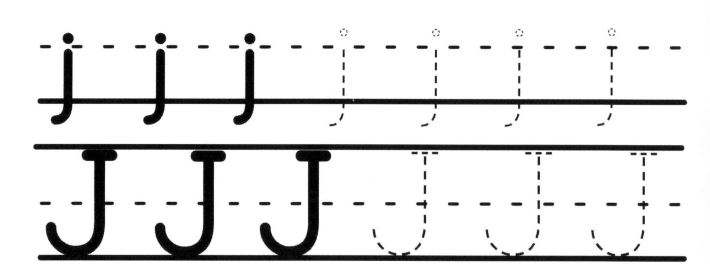

j j j

J J J

kentrosaurus

kentrosaurus

k k k k k k k

K K K K K K K

leptoceratops

leptoceratops

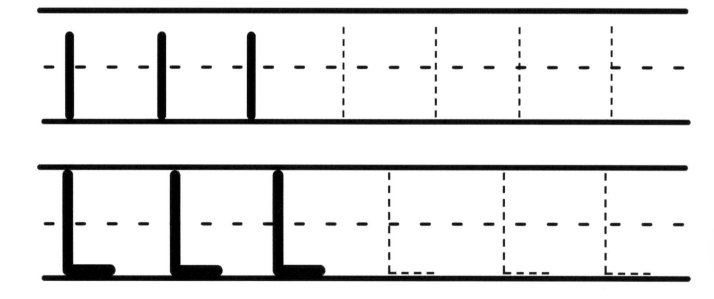

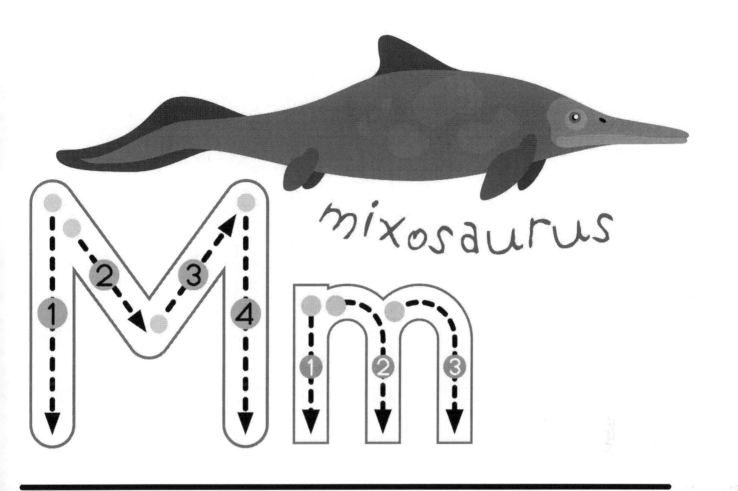

mixosaurus

mixosaurus

mmm mmm m

MM M-M-M-M-M

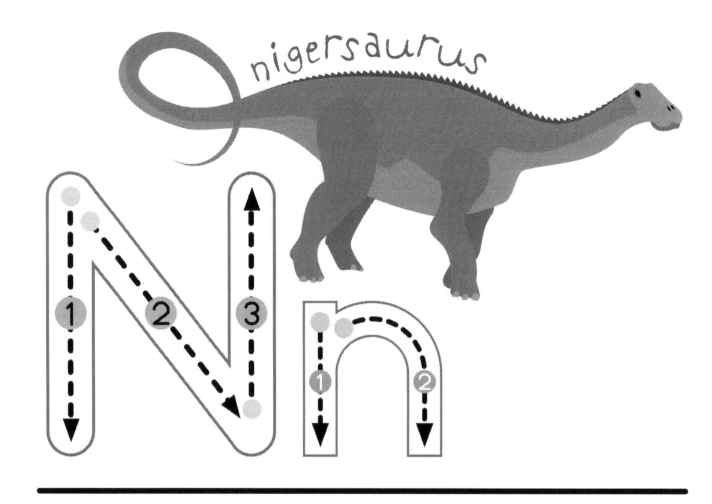

nigersaurus

n n n n n n n

N N N N N N N

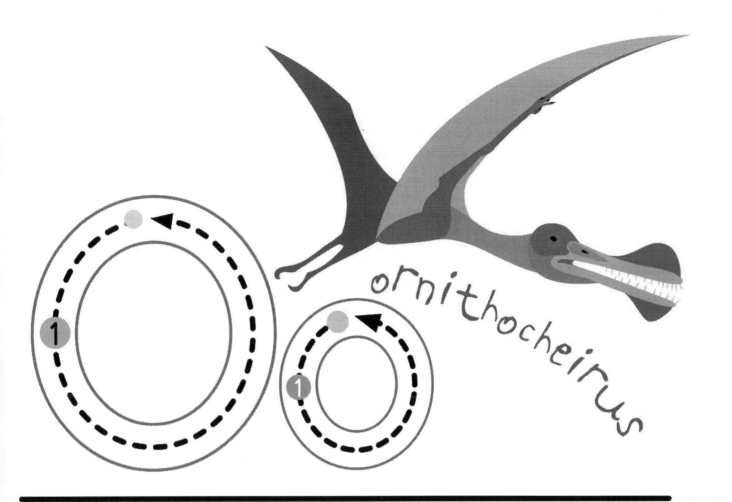

ornithocheirus

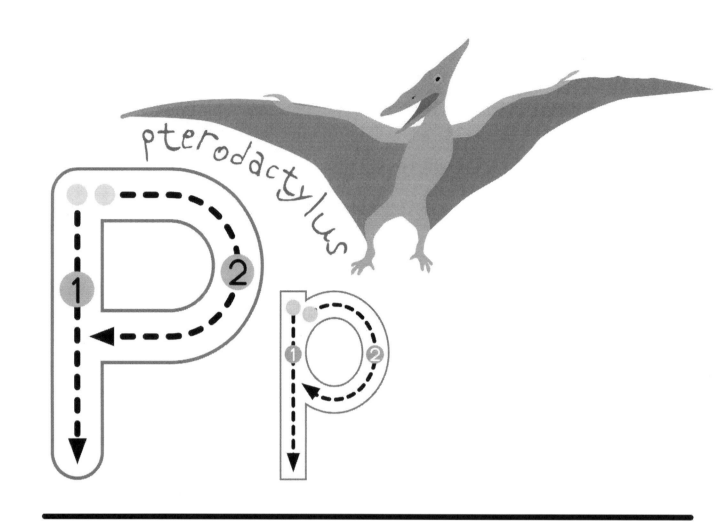

pterodactylus

p p p p p p p

P P P P P P P

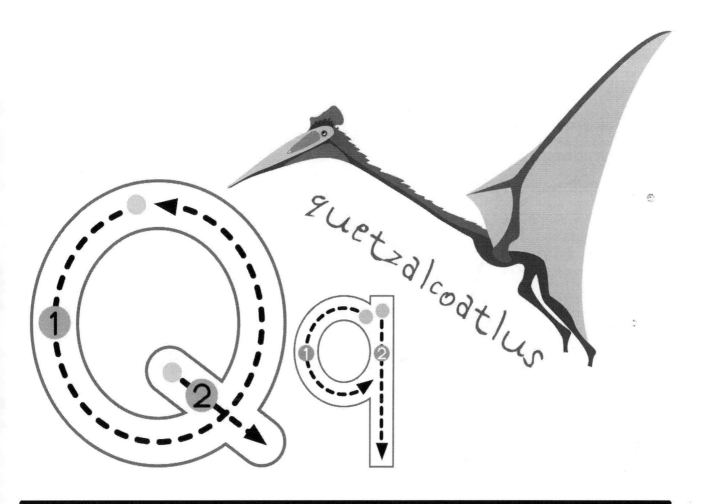

quetzalcoatlus

quetzalcoatlus

q q q q q q q

Q Q Q Q Q Q

t - Rex

---

t - rex

r r r r r r r r r

R R R R R R R

stegosaurus

stegosaurus

s s s s s s s

S S S S S S

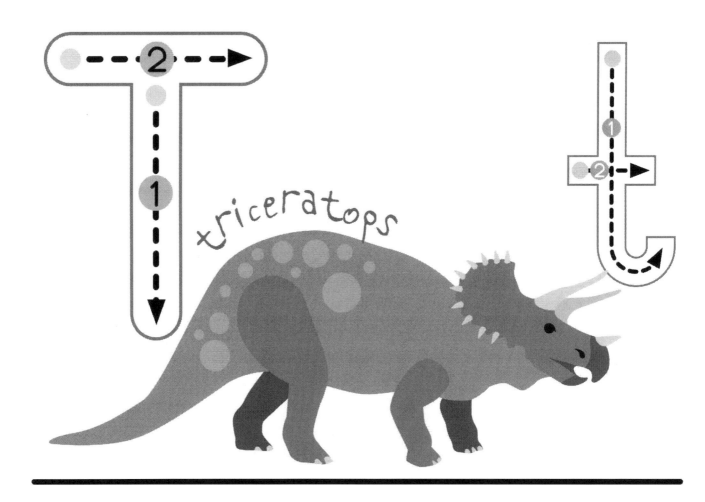

triceratops

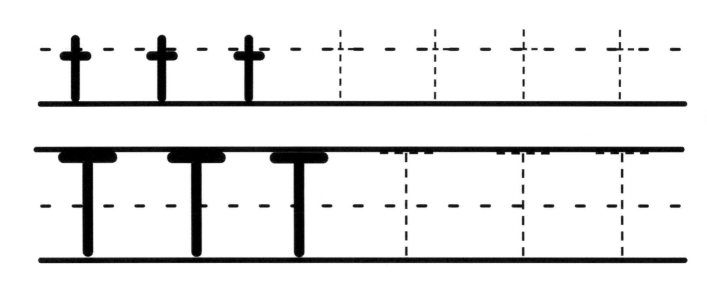

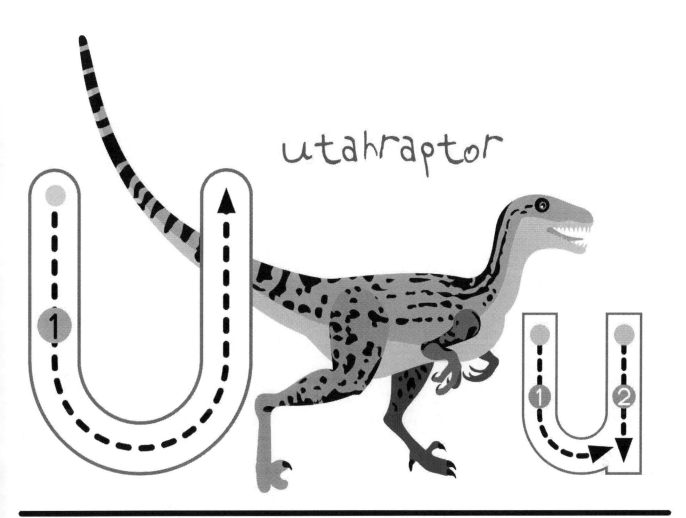

utahraptor

utahraptor

u u u U U U U U

U U U U U U U U

velociraptor

velociraptor

V V V V V V V

V V V V V V V

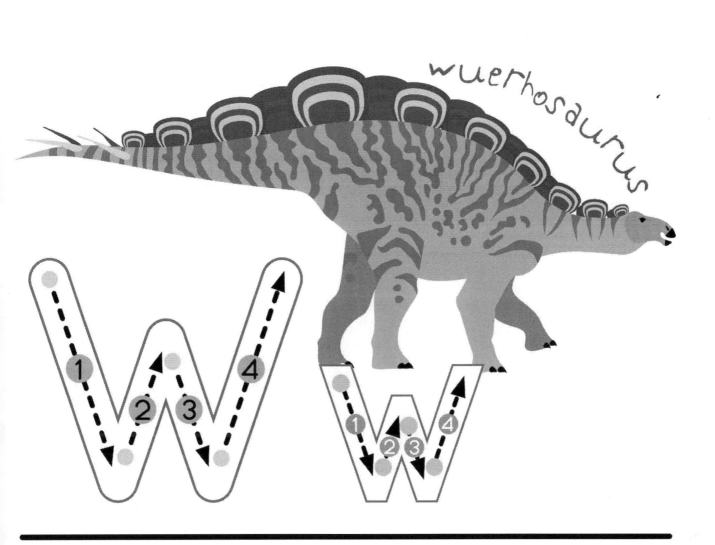

wuerhosaurus

wuerhosaurus

W W W   W W W

WW W W

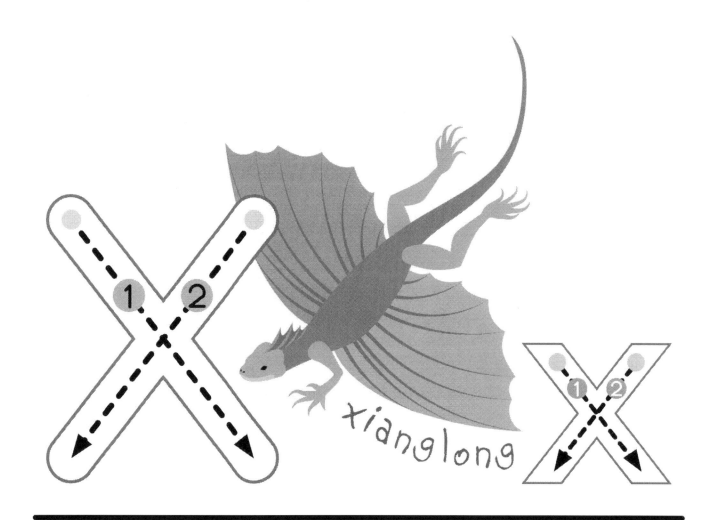

xianglong

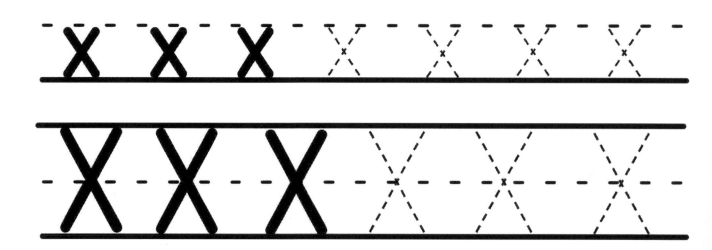

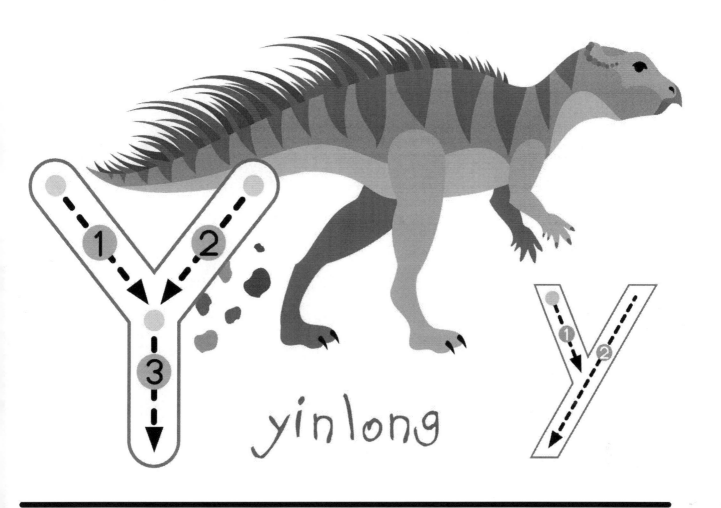

yinlong

yinlong

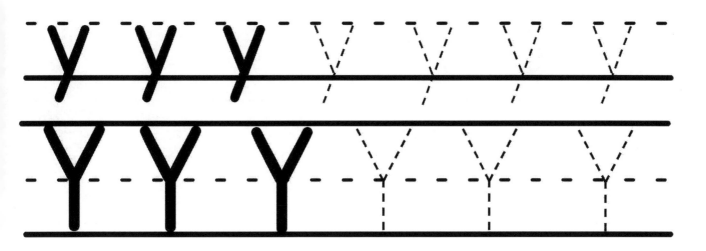

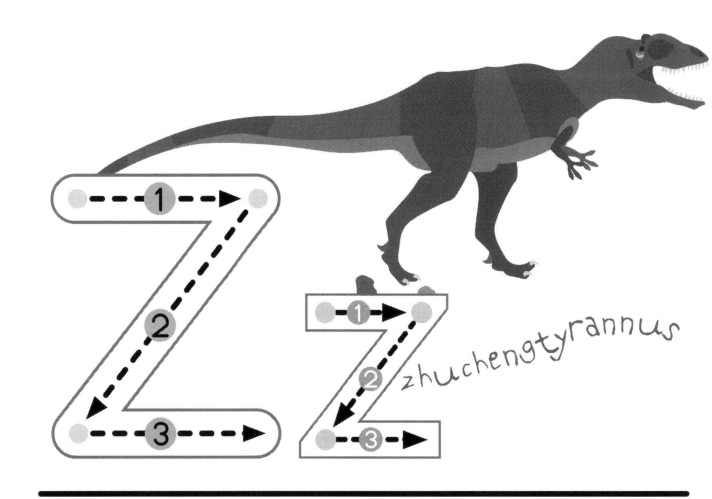

zhuchengtyrannus

zhuchengtyrannus

z z z z z z z

Z Z Z Z Z Z Z

Sight Words
A - Z

after after after

and and and

at at at

all all all

again again

away away

been been

before before

big big

call   call   call

come   come

could   could

city city city

close close

cut cut cut

dad _ _ _ _ dad

didn't _ _ didn't

down _ down

for   for   for

friend   friend

from   from

get   get   get

goes   goes

good   good

grow   grow

girl   girl   girl

group   group

have   have

him   him

how   how

his his his

her her her

had had had

I

is

into

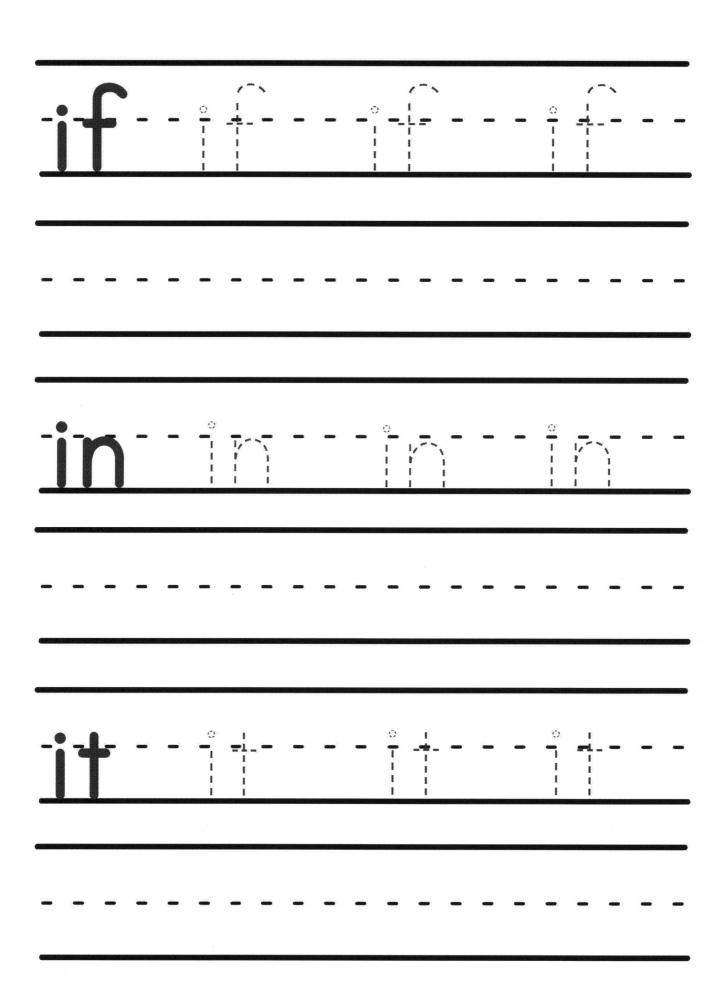

like   like

little   little

love   love

make make

mum mum

my my my

not not not

now now

next next

on   on   on

out   out   out

over   over

one one one

our our our

own own

page   page

play   play

point   point

part   part

place   place

put   put   put

run run run

river river

read read

said said

she she she

so so so

the the the

there there

they they

that   that

then   then

to   to to to

upon   upon   upon

up   up   up

use   use   use

very   very

was   was

we   we   we

were   were

what   what

where where

you   you

your   your

year   year

Bonus

Ankylosaurs

Caudipteryx

Iguanadon

Jobaria

Triceratops

Velociraptor

MORE KIDS' ACTIVITY BOOKS FROM US
https://k-imagine-pub.com/

Kids' Activity Workbook Subscribe

Get New Update,
Book Giveaway,
Free Book for Kids
and Promotion

http://bit.ly/act_book_4_kids

Made in the USA
Middletown, DE
29 June 2020